GOOGLE MEET
MADE EASY

Video Conferencing The Easy Way

By James Bernstein

Bernstein, James
Google Meet Made Easy
Book 18 in the Computers Made Easy series

For more information on reproducing sections of this book or sales of this book,
go to www.onlinecomputertips.com

Contents

Introduction

Thanks to modern technology and the fact that all of our devices are Internet enabled means that keeping connected with friends, family and coworkers is even easier than ever. We can use our computers, tablets and smartphones to do things such as make video calls, hold meetings and have presentations in addition to sending emails and text messages.

Fortunately, there are many ways to go about performing these tasks yet unfortunately you will need to choose the platform you are going to use to do this because you will need to decide on which method (or software) you will be using. It's important to choose a platform that is easy to use and also something the people you will be communicating with can also use without having too much of a learning curve in case they are not too tech savvy.

Just like with most software, there are a few vendors who dominate the market for their respective types of applications such as Microsoft does for operating systems (Windows) and word processors (Microsoft Word). You have most likely heard of other software such as Skype that allows video calls and GoToMeeting which is commonly used in the business sector for hosting online meetings that can be accessed from anywhere you have an Internet connection.

Ever since Zoom started to dominate the video conference scene with their popular online meeting service, other vendors have been scrambling to get their own piece of the video conferencing pie. And since Google is one of the largest providers of online services, it only made sense that they came out with their own service to compete with Zoom and hopefully steal some of their users in the process. If you would like to learn more about Zoom then check out my book titled **Zoom Made Easy**. https://www.amazon.com/dp/B088B96YNK

Although Google Meet doesn't have all the features that Zoom does, it's still a very powerful tool for those who want to host video calls and conferences. For most of us, it has enough features to get the job done and since it's a Google service, of course it will integrate into other Google products such as Gmail and the Google Calendar making it easy to access assuming you are a Google user.

The goal of this book is to get you up and running with Meet and show you how to host meetings and calls as well as go over all of the basic features of Meet and also some of the more advanced options. I will also go over the configuration

Introduction

settings so you will know how to customize Meet to make it work just the way you want it to work. So on that note, let's get the communication channels open!

Chapter 1 – What is Google Meet?

If you are reading this book then you have either tried to use Google Meet and want to improve your skills with the app or you are thinking about using Meet for your online video calls and meetings. Or maybe you are just wanting to compare Meet to other collaboration services like Zoom or Microsoft Teams.

Regardless of the reason you are reading this book, the end result should be that you have a better understanding of how Google Meet works and if it's the right collaboration service for you.

Overview
Google Meet is a fairly simple application that still offers some powerful features. Sure it's not a complex as other applications such as Microsoft Teams for example which offers many more features. But the goal of Teams is to keep it simple while still giving you all the tools you need to get the job done.

Google Meet was originally available to those who were subscribed to the *Google G Suite* service which is a suite of web applications created by Google for businesses that offers an all in one service to perform tasks such as send emails, store files, share documents and keep things organized with online calendars. Once Zoom took off with their free collaboration service, Google decided to follow suit and make a free version of Meet as well.

The main purpose of Google Meet is to hold video conference calls or online meetings with friends, family or coworkers. This can be done using your computer, smartphone or tablet. Once you join a meeting you will then be able to see anyone who has a camera attached to their computer, assuming they have it enabled within Meet to allow you to see them. You will also be able to hear everyone who is attending the meeting assuming they have some type of microphone or are calling in on their phone. Figure 1.1 (image courtesy of Google) shows an example of a Google Meet call with several attendees. Even though it looks like there are only 4 people in the meeting there are actually more, and I will show you how to change the views to show more or less of your participants later in the book.

Figure 1.1

Another thing you can do in Meet is share your screen so others on the call can see what you are working on as if they were sitting right there with you at your desk. This comes in handy because letting someone see what you are working on is usually easier than trying to explain it. Other people can share what they are working on as well.

If you have something that you would like to share with others, yet you don't want to disrupt the meeting in progress then you can use the chat feature to send a message to other people. The chat feature is similar to instant messaging apps and you can think of it as sending text messages to others in the meeting.

I will be going over these features in more detail throughout the book but as you can see there is nothing overly complicated about the service and you don't need to be a tech expert in order to use it.

Google Accounts

Since Google Meet is a Google product it makes sense that they will want you to have a Google account in order to use it. Once you have a Google account, you can use this account to sign in to most if not all of the Google products\applications that you use. For example, you can use the same account to post videos on YouTube (since it's owned by Google), write emails with Gmail and edit documents using Google Docs.

If you are interested in learning more about the applications that Google has to offer then you should check out my book titled Google Apps Made Easy to learn more!
https://www.amazon.com/dp/1798114992

If you are going to be joining someone else's meeting you don't need to have a Google account but if you want to host your own meetings then you will need to have a Google account to sign in with. Fortunately, signing up for a Google account is free and fairly easy to do.

To get your own Google account all you need to do is open your web browser and navigate to *google.com* and click on the *Sign in* button, which might seem like a strange thing to do since you don't have an account to sign into but it will get you there.

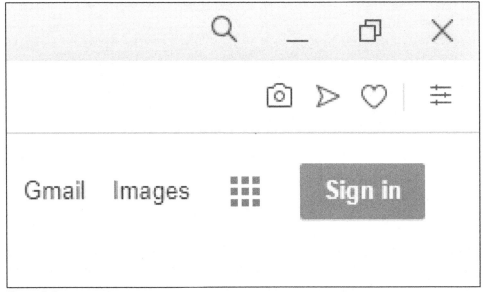

Figure 1.1

Next, you will see a screen where you can enter in your email address to log in if you did have a Google account, but you want to click on the link at the bottom that says *Create account* and then choose *For myself*.

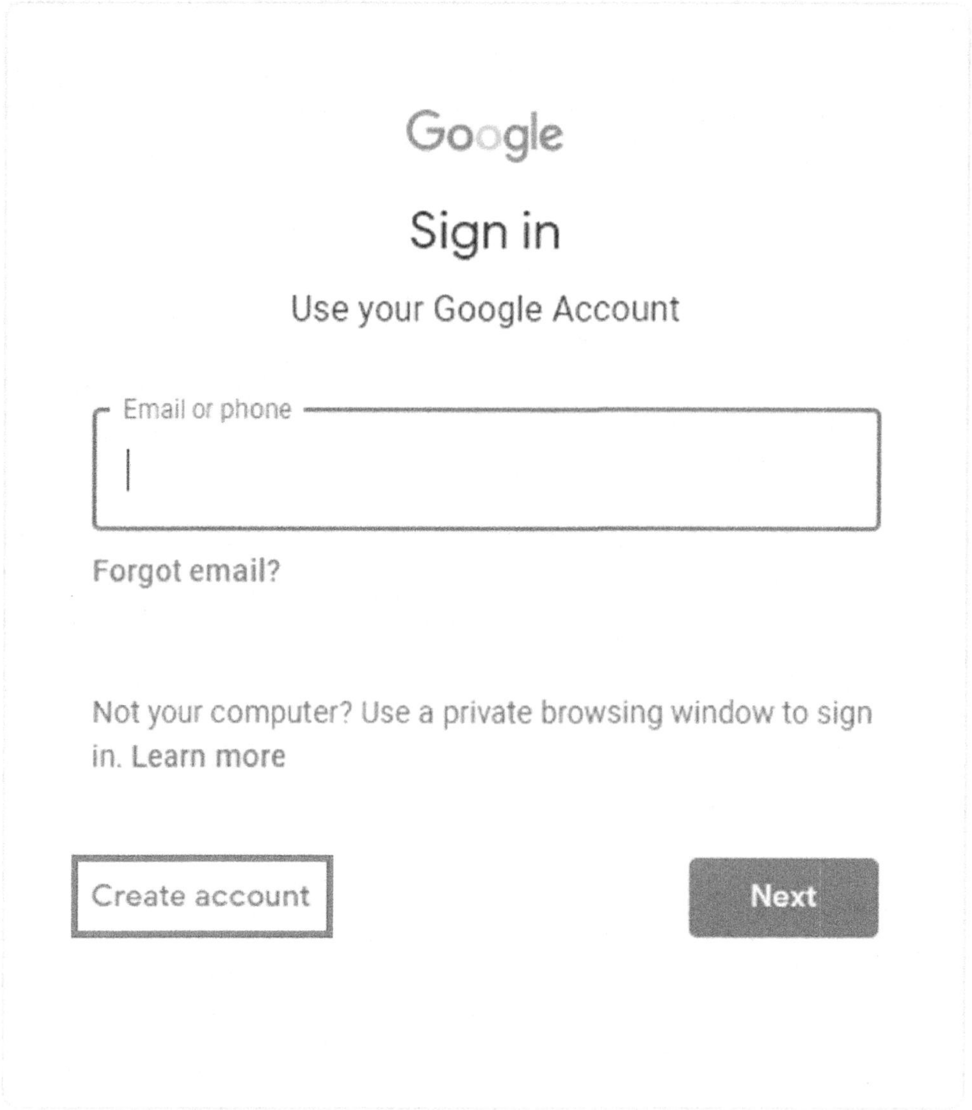

Google

Sign in

Use your Google Account

Email or phone

Forgot email?

Not your computer? Use a private browsing window to sign in. Learn more

Create account   Next

Figure 1.2

Next, you will be asked to enter your first and last name, and it's up to you if you want to use your real name or not. Then Google will suggest a username based on the name you typed in. So for my example, I entered Todd Simms and it suggested I use *todd3674@gmail.com* for my email address but I am going to try something a little more unique by changing the username to tsimms. As you can see in figure 1.4 that *tsimms@gmail.com* is already taken so I will have to try something else.

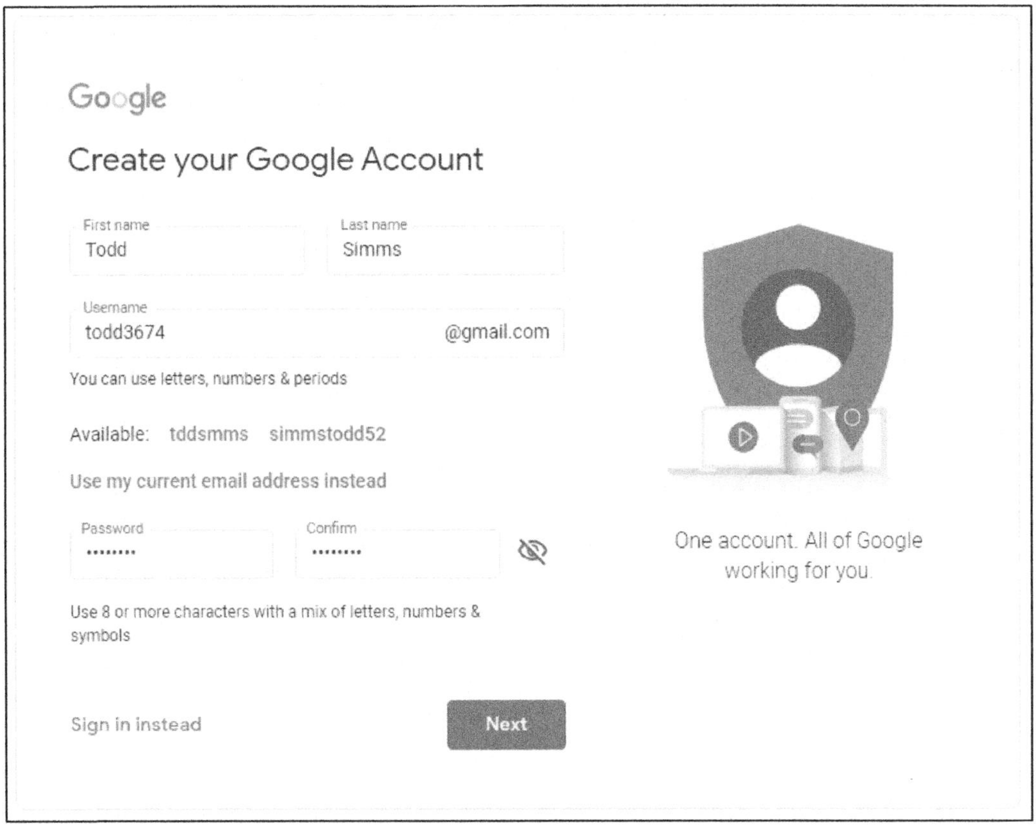

Figure 1.3

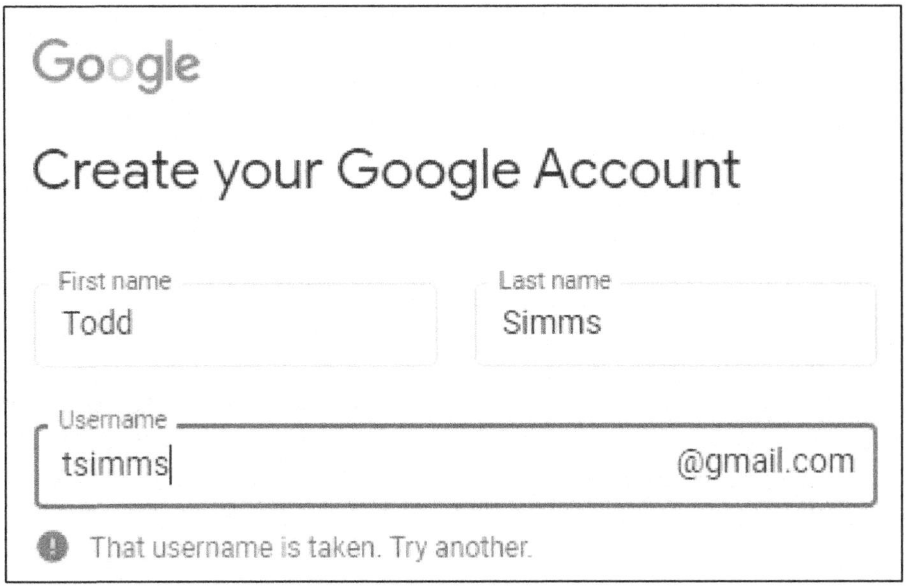

Figure 1.4

After a few tries, I was able to get toddsimms007 to work so now I can look like I am a secret agent like James Bond!

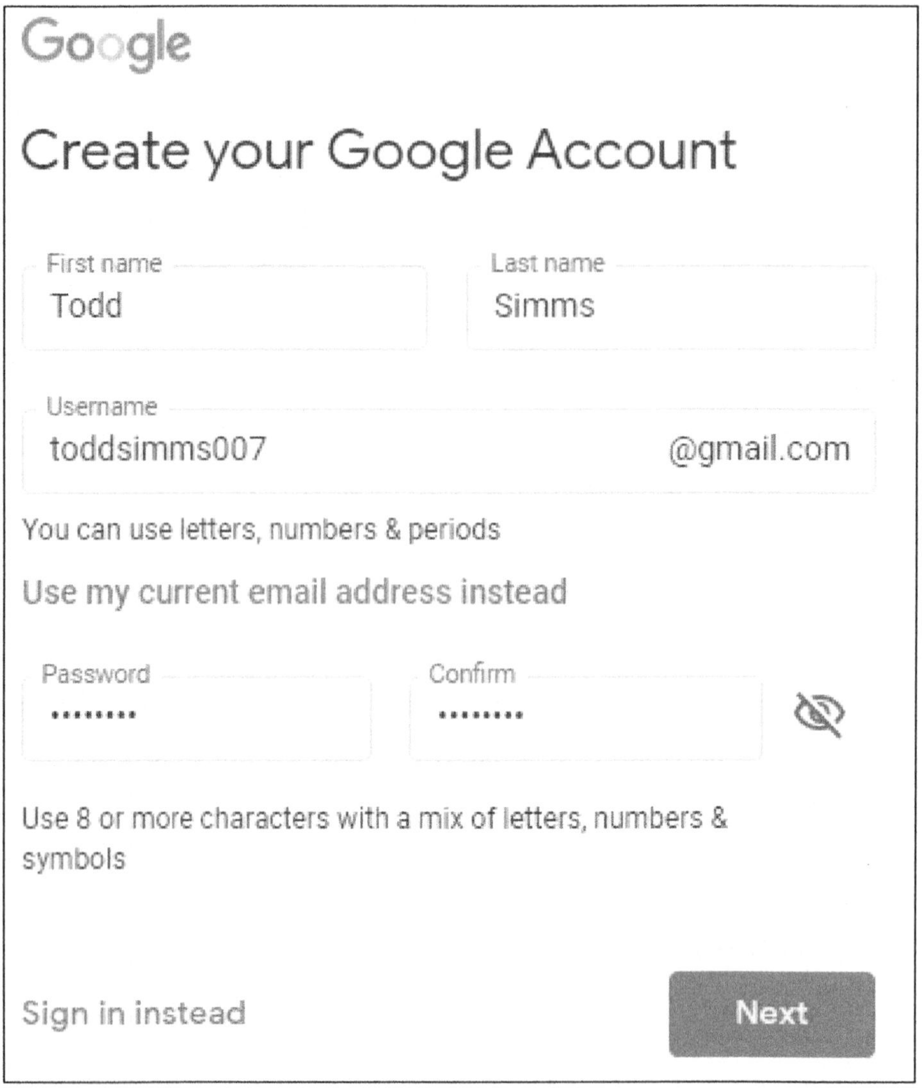

Figure 1.5

You might have noticed in figure 1.5 that it says *Use my current email address instead*. This means that you can sign up for a Google account with a non-Google email address that you already have if you do not wish to have an actual Google (Gmail) email address. Next I will make up a secure password and click on *Next*.

Next, you will have some optional information that you can tell Google about to help secure your account. If you ever forget your password you can have Google do things such as send you a text message to help you recover it or create a new one or have it send an email to a recovery email address which is some other email address that you use. The reason for entering your birthday is to prove that you are old enough to access any Google content that might have an age requirement such as certain YouTube videos.

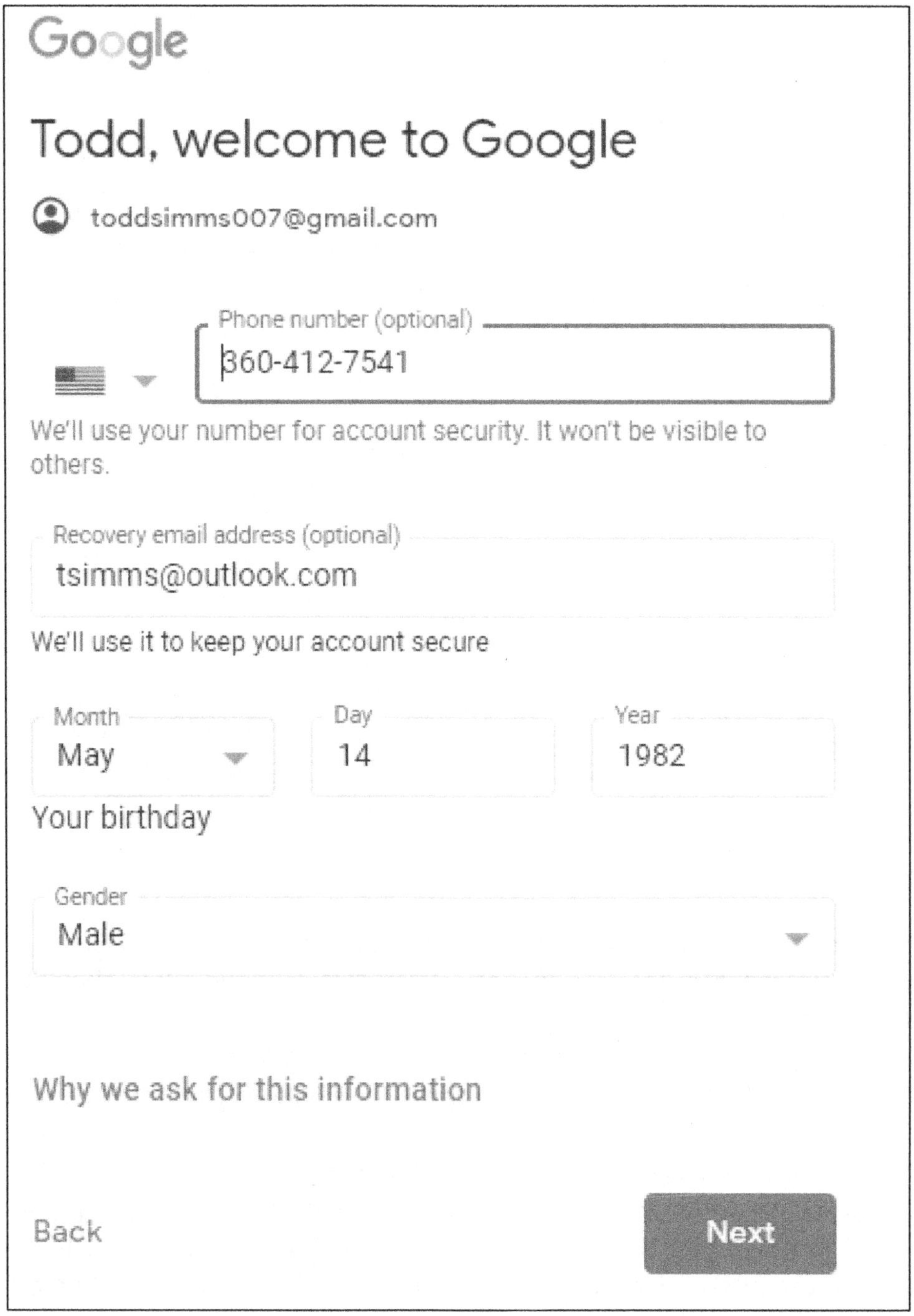

Google

Todd, welcome to Google

toddsimms007@gmail.com

Phone number (optional)
360-412-7541

We'll use your number for account security. It won't be visible to others.

Recovery email address (optional)
tsimms@outlook.com

We'll use it to keep your account secure

Month	Day	Year
May	14	1982

Your birthday

Gender
Male

Why we ask for this information

Back   Next

Figure 1.6

When I click on *Next* it will want to verify the phone number I entered by sending me a text message but since I just made up this phone number I will click on *Not now*.

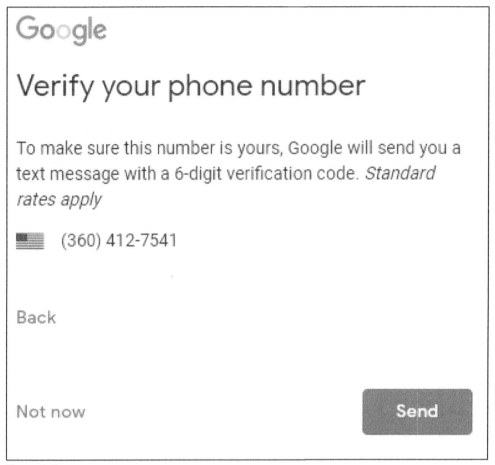

Figure 1.7

Then you will be shown a page with a bunch of privacy terms that you will need to agree to by clicking the *I agree* button. After this step you will then be automatically logged into your new Google account and will notice at the top right of the Google webpage that you will have a letter corresponding to your first name and if you click on it then you will see information about your account (figure 1.8).

Clicking on *Manage your Google Account* will take you to a page where you can adjust things such as privacy and security settings and online storage options (figure 1.9). I won't go into these settings now but feel free to poke around on your own. You can also click on the camera icon to change your account image from a letter to an actual photo of yourself or anything else you might want to use. You can upload a picture from your computer and crop it to make it look the way you like which I think I will do since the T looks kind of boring.

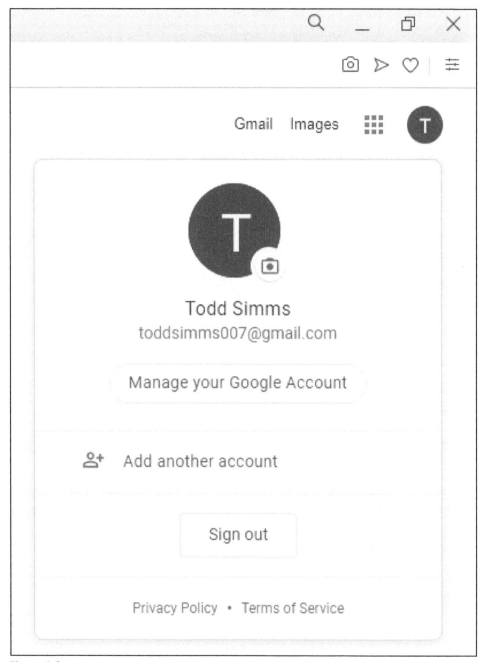

Figure 1.8

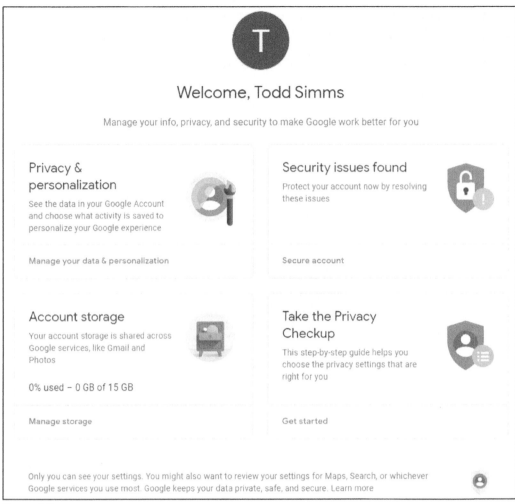

Figure 1.9

Now that you have your Google account setup you can click on your account picture (or letter) and here you will see all of the Google apps that are available to you such as Maps, YouTube, Gmail and of course Meet (figure 1.10). You can click and drag the apps around to put them in any order you like.

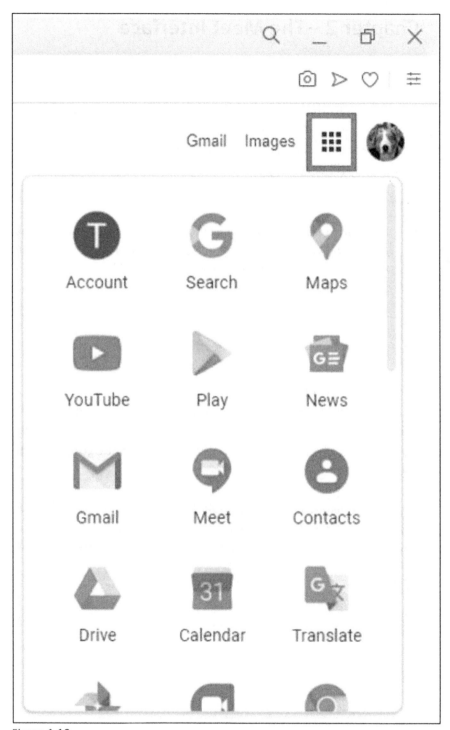

Figure 1.10

Chapter 2 – The Meet Interface

The Google Meet interface is fairly basic and easy to navigate so if you are new to online meetings and video calls then you should find that you are able to get used to how things work fairly quickly. Meet has the same look and feel as the other popular online meeting services such as Zoom for example which is actually more complicated than Meet yet still very easy to use.

If you are interested in learning more about how Zoom works and also how it compares to Google Meet then you should check out my book titled **Zoom Made Easy** to learn more!
https://www.amazon.com/dp/B088B96YNK

Getting to the Meet Website and Logging In

The first thing you need to do in order to start using Google Meet is to go to the Google Meet website. You can get there by opening the app from your Google apps like I showed you back in Chapter one or simply by typing **meet.google.com/** into your web browser.

Once you get to the Google Meet website you will be asked if you wish to start (host) a meeting or join a meeting that someone else is hosting. For now I will start a meeting by clicking on the *Start a meeting* button just so I can get into the Meet interface.

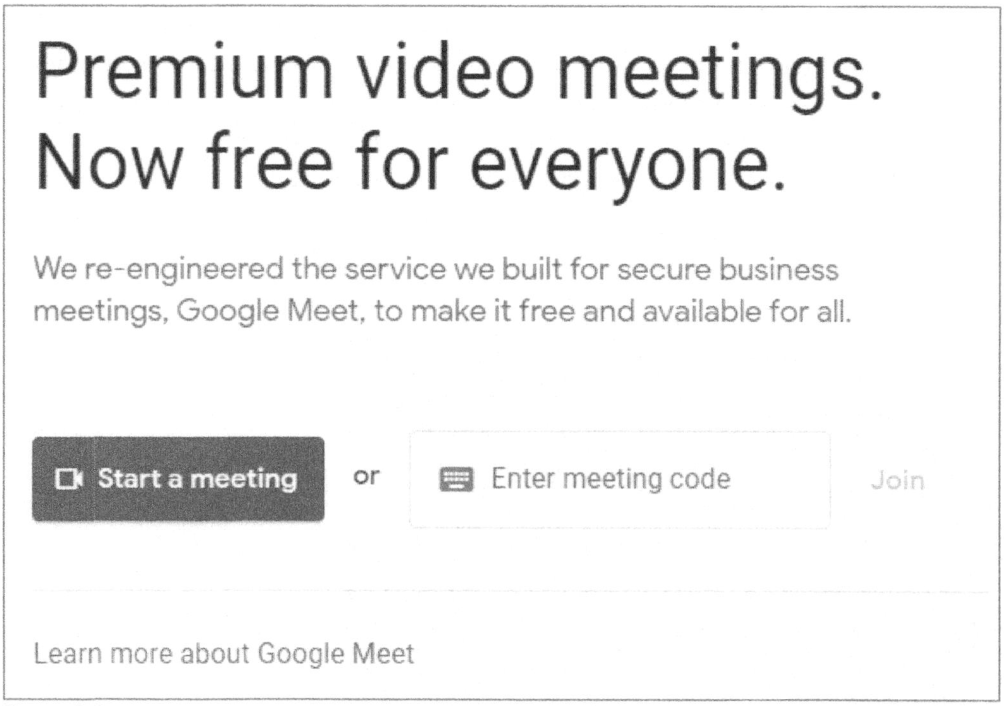

Premium video meetings.
Now free for everyone.
We re-engineered the service we built for secure business meetings, Google Meet, to make it free and available for all.
Start a meeting
or
Enter meeting code
Join
Learn more about Google Meet

Figure 2.1

You will then most likely be prompted to give Meet access to use your microphone for meetings and video calls so others can hear you talking. Depending on what web browser you are using the notification might look a little different from mine.

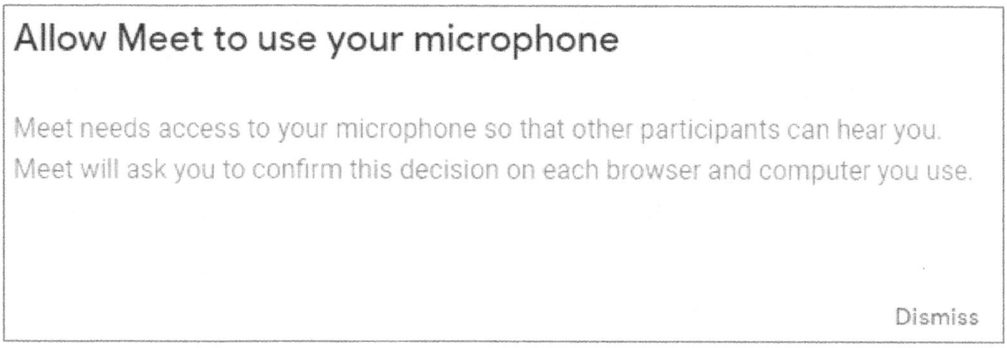

Allow Meet to use your microphone
Meet needs access to your microphone so that other participants can hear you.
Meet will ask you to confirm this decision on each browser and computer you use.
Dismiss

Figure 2.2

meet.google.com wants to
Show notifications
Allow
Block

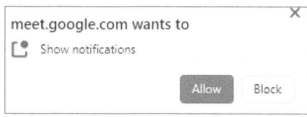

Figure 2.3

When you first start a meeting you will be shown your video display as seen through your camera so you can make sure everything looks correct. If you don't have a camera connected to your computer then you will see something that looks similar to figure 2.4. This doesn't mean that you can't use Meet but does mean that nobody will be able to see you during the meeting which might be fine with you anyway. If you do have a camera and it has been recognized by Meet then you should see yourself in the video assuming you are sitting in front of your camera.

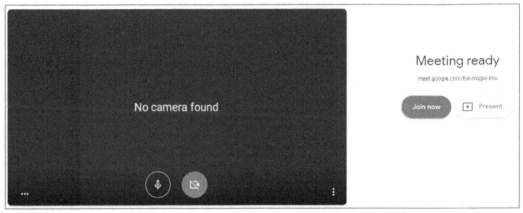

Figure 2.4

When you are sure that things look good then you can click the *Join now* button to officially begin the meeting. Clicking on *Present* will give you an option to share your computer screen with the others in the meeting. I will be going over presenting\screen sharing in Chapter 4.

When the meeting first starts you will be presented with an option to copy the link to your meeting that you can send to others or add other people right on the spot. I will be going over meeting invitations in Chapter 3. Since I don't want to invite any other people to my meeting at the moment I will just click the X at the top right of the *Add others* screen.

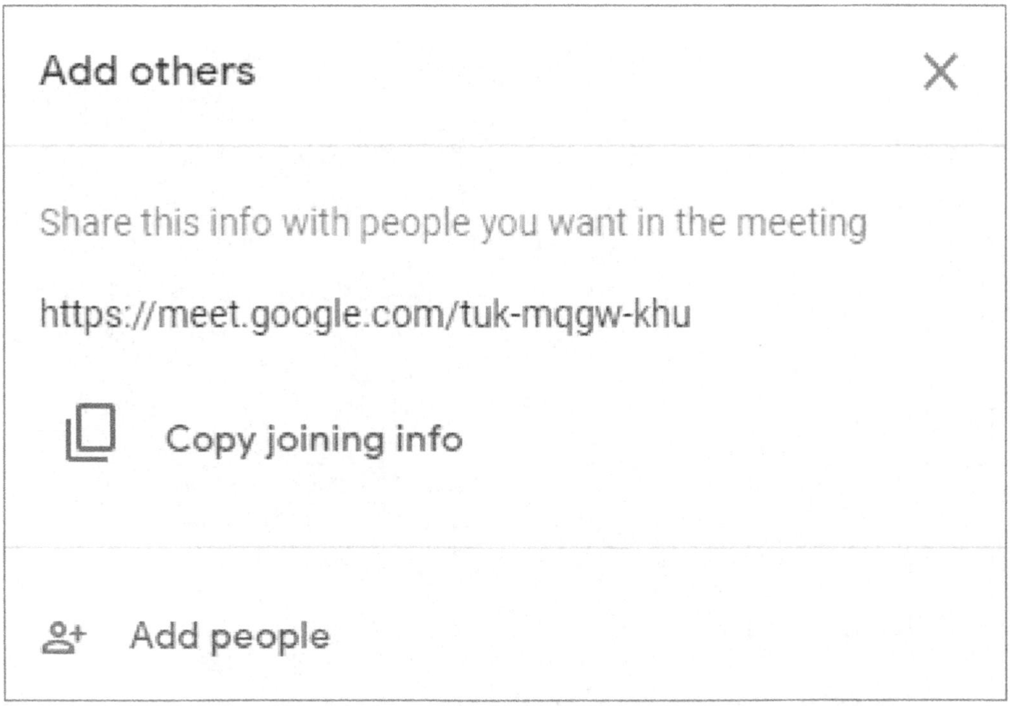

Figure 2.5

Now I will see the main Meet interface and as you can see from figure 2.6, there is not much to it. Since I don't have a camera on this computer, Meet will show the profile picture from my Google account. It will also use your profile picture if you choose to turn your camera off during the meeting.

Down at the bottom of the window you will see basic controls such as the microphone icon which is used to mute and unmute your microphone, the phone icon which is used to hang up the call and the video camera icon which is used to show and hide your video (figure 2.7).

Figure 2.6

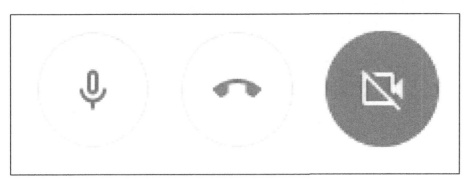

Figure 2.7

Clicking on *Meeting details* at the lower left of the screen will give you information about your meeting such as the link to your meeting. It will also give you an option to copy the meeting information so you can paste it into an email to send to others you wish to invite to your meeting. There is also an option for attaching files that I will be going over in Chapter 4.

Figure 2.8

If you were to click on the 3 vertical dots at the lower right corner of the screen as seen in figure 2.6 you will get some additional options having the window show in full screen mode or getting some additional help. I will be going over these choices later in the book.

At the top right of the screen you will see the participant list, chat feature and your profile picture. I will be going over these in more detail later as well.

Figure 2.9

Joining a Meeting
Not only can you host your own meetings, but you also have the capability to join a meeting that was set up by someone else and the process of joining another person's meeting is very simple.

In order to join a meeting, you will need a link or meeting ID from the person who is hosting the meeting. Normally they would send you this information in an email or even something like a text message or instant messenger chat.

Once you get the link all you need to do is click on it and you will be brought to the Google Meet web page. The interface will look the same as it did when you started your own meeting except the green button will say *Ask to join* rather than *Join now*.

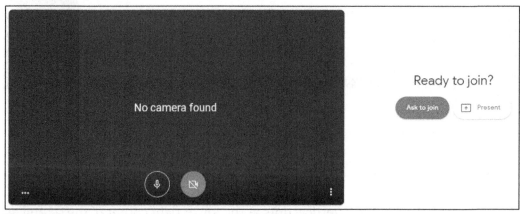

Figure 2.10

When you click on Ask to join you will get a message telling you that Meet is asking the host to give you permission to join his or her meeting.

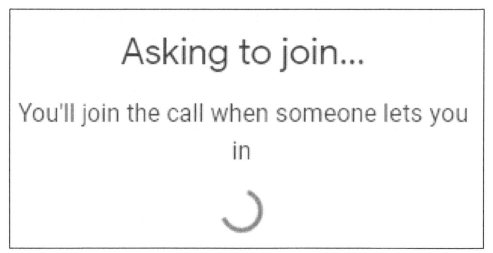

Figure 2.11

Figure 2.12 shows what the host will see and then they can either admit you to their meeting or deny you access.

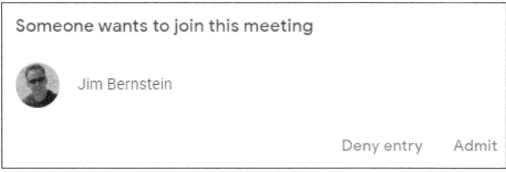

Figure 2.12

Then once they admit you to their meeting it will show that you have joined on their end and then you will be able to participate with all the other people who have joined the meeting.

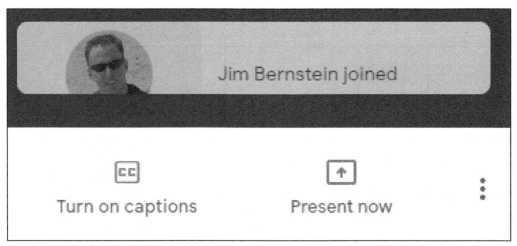

Figure 2.13

Another way to join a meeting is from the Google Meet home page where it says *Enter meeting code.*

Figure 2.14

Here you can paste in the URL\address from the invitation that you got in your email which was taken from the Meeting details section from the host. Then just click on Join and you will be ready to go. You can also just enter the last characters from the link which is actually the meeting code (*axm-kduk-eeo* in my example).

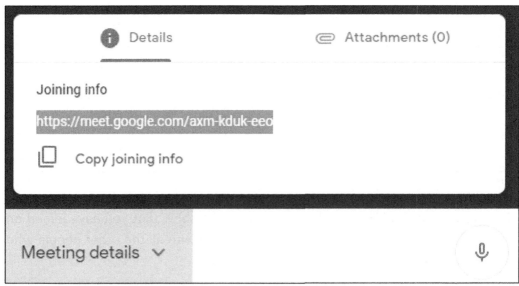

Figure 2.15

Figure 2.16

Installing the Google Meet App on your Smartphone or Tablet

Since many people prefer to use their smartphone or tablet rather than a desktop or laptop computer, it makes sense that Google would make an app (application) for mobile devices so you can host and join meetings from anywhere that you have an internet connection.

You can install the Google Meet app on your phone or tablet just like you would any other app. If you have an iPhone you would go to the *App Store* and search for Google Meet. And if you have an Android device you would go to the *Play Store* and do the same thing.

Since I have an Android smartphone I will be using the Play Store method for my example. Once you find the Google Meet app, simply tap on *Install* and let the application do its thing and install itself on your device.

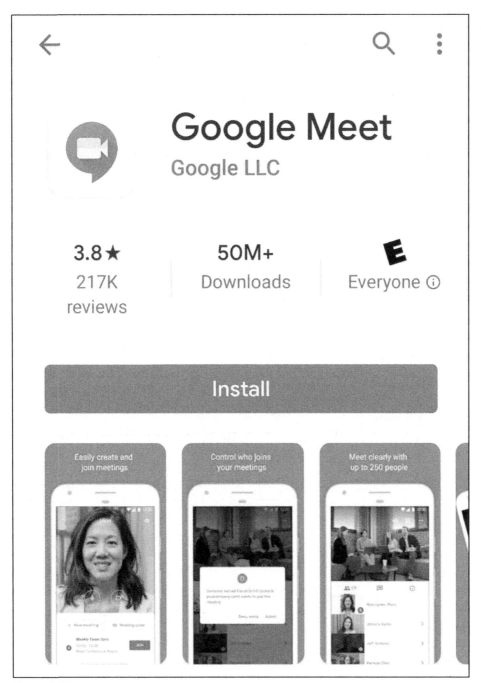

Figure 2.17

When the installation is complete you can tap on the *Open* button or look for the green Meet icon on your home screen or another screen on your device.

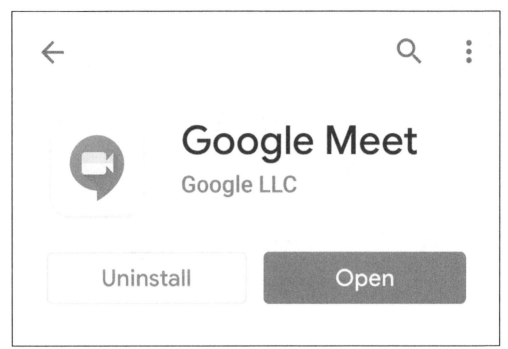

Figure 2.18

When you open the Meet app the first time you might get a message similar to figure 2.19 that will allow you to read the terms of service and privacy policy if you desire to do so. I don't know of anyone who actually reads those things but maybe we should!

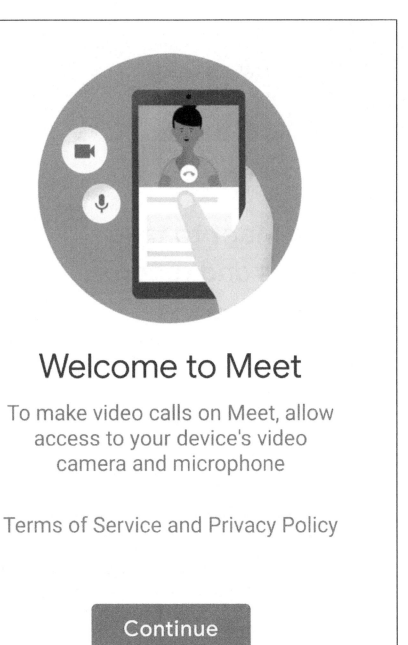

Figure 2.19

After you tap on *Continue* you will be asked to give Meet permission to access your camera a microphone so it can display video and transmit audio during your meetings.

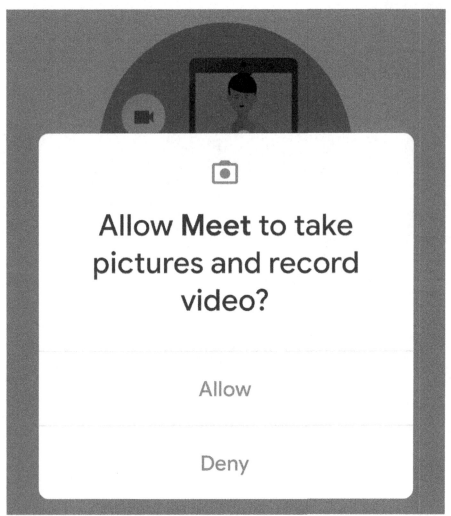

Figure 2.20

Next, you will be presented with a screen where you can start a meeting or join someone else's meeting depending on what you are trying to do. Tapping on *Meeting Code* will allow you to enter the code given to you by the person hosting the meeting so you can join their meeting.

At the bottom of the screen in figure 2.21, you will see that it says *Swipe up to see your meetings* and this can be used to view any meetings you might have scheduled in case you were wondering what you have coming up in the future.

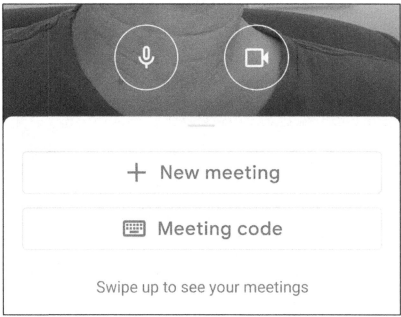

Figure 2.21

If you were to tap on *New meeting* then you will be given a link to your new meeting that you can share with others to invite them to join. You can share the link via email, text, chat or another type of app you have installed on your device.

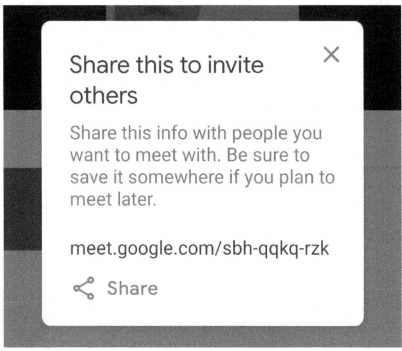

Figure 2.22

Once you are in your meeting and someone else tries to join you will get a message similar to figure 2.23 where you can grant or deny them access to your meeting.

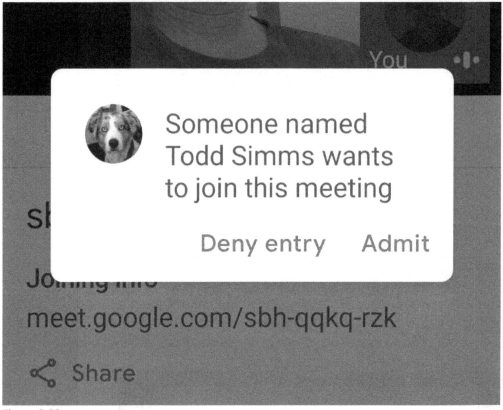

Figure 2.23

Once they have joined your meeting you will see their video if they have it enabled, otherwise you will see their profile picture (if they have one) as shown in figure 2.24.

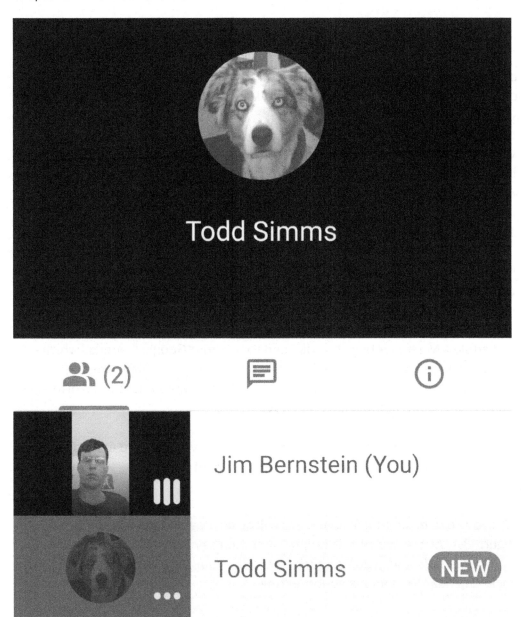

Figure 2.24

Now you will be able to use meet in a similar fashion to how you use it on your desktop computer. Things will look a little different, but the basic functionality will be about the same and it should be pretty easy to figure out if you are used to the desktop version.

Chapter 3 – Hosting and Joining Meetings

Now that you hopefully have a better understanding of what you can do with Google Meet and how to navigate around its interface, it's time to start hosing and joining some meetings.

I went over this process a little bit in the last chapter but will now go over it again while getting into more detail about how to host your own meetings and join meetings that others are hosting.

Scheduling a Meeting
In the last chapter, I showed you how easy it was to start a meeting on the spot with just the click of a mouse but now I would like to go over how to schedule a meeting since most of the time you will need to make sure that everyone who is going to be participating in the meeting has the time to attend.

To schedule a Meet meeting you will need to use your Google Calendar which you will have included with your Google account. You can go to **calendar.google.com/** to access yours while you are logged into your Google account. You can also log in from here if you are not logged in already.

Before I show you how to schedule a meeting from your Google Calendar I want to show you a shortcut you can use from the Meet homepage to do the same thing.

When you go to *meet.google.com* there will be an area that has a graphic as shown in figure 3.1. At the top of this graphic it should say *Schedule a Google meeting from Google Calendar*. You can click here with your mouse to be taken to your Google Calendar to schedule your meeting.

Since technology is always changing you might find that things you are used to seeing online and with your software have also been changed or rearranged. So if you see something in this book and it doesn't look quite the same in your own experience, then this is the reason why.

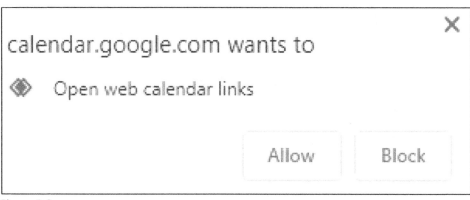

+ Schedule a video meeting from Google Calendar

Figure 3.1

When you have Meet open your calendar for the first time you might get a couple of popups from your computer asking you to give Google Calendar permission to access web calendar links and show you notifications on your computer as seen in figures 3.2 through 3.4. Of course all of these notifications may vary depending on your computer and what operating system you are using.

calendar.google.com wants to   ✕

◈   Open web calendar links

                                        Allow   Block

Figure 3.2

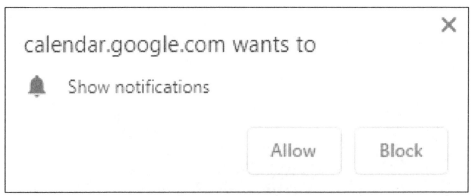

Figure 3.3

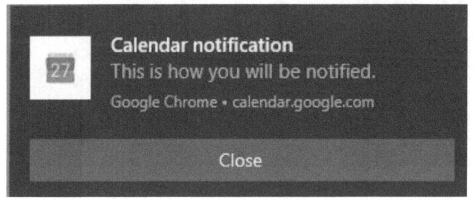

Figure 3.4

Next, you should be taken to your Google Calendar and right to the current date and you will be able to schedule your meeting from here. As you can see in figure 3.5, there are many options to choose from when scheduling a meeting and you can even schedule a Zoom meeting from here instead if you would rather use Zoom or if your participants are more comfortable using Zoom.

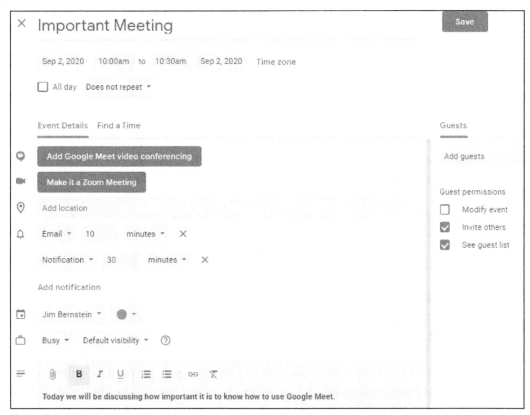

Figure 3.5

Now I would like to go over all the options you can configure when scheduling a meeting using your Google Calendar.

- **Date & Time** – Here is where you choose the date and time for the meeting as well as its duration. If you check the box that says *All day* then it will be scheduled for the entire day.

- **Repeating Meetings** – If this meeting is one that needs to be repeated every Friday or on the first Wednesday of the month for example then you can set that here, so you don't need to come in and reconfigure the meeting for each occurrence. Rather Google will add it to your calendar for you at the intervals you specify.

- **Location** – Here you can add in a location such as Conference Room 3 for example. You will probably leave this blank since your participants will most likely all be joining from different locations. You can still put something funny like Hawaii just to get a laugh if you want.

- **Notifications** – Here is where you set reminders for your upcoming meetings, so you don't forget that you have them. You can have Google Meet send you email reminders and well as popup notifications on your computer when it's almost time for the meeting to start. You can have the notifications be minutes, hours, days or weeks in advance.

- **Calendar Selection** – If you have more than one Google Calendar then here is where you choose which one you want the meeting to be added to. You can have multiple calendars for personal, school, work and so on.

- **Availability** – When you schedule a meeting you can have your calendar show you as busy so that way others that can see your calendar will know not to schedule anything on that date and time with you.

- **Meeting Details** – Here you can add a description of what the meeting is about as well as add attachments such as documents to the meeting that you can use during the meeting.

When you click on the *Find a Time* section of the calendar, you will be shown your calendar and any events that you have for the time period you are looking at. You can have your calendar displayed in a day or week view to see what you have going on. Figure 3.6 shows that I have an event on Friday the 4th from 3:00 to 5:00 so I know not to schedule any meetings for that date and time.

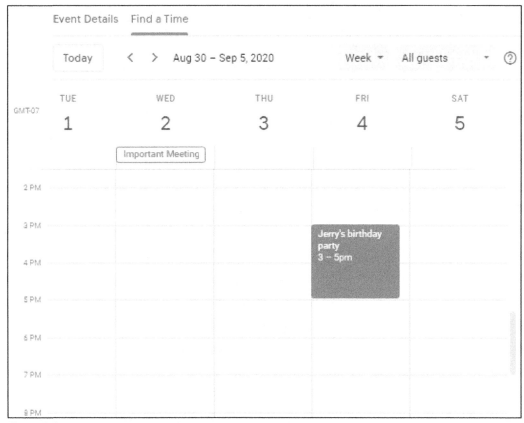

Figure 3.6

When you are done choosing your date, time and options then you can click on the *Add Google Meet video conferencing* button as shown in figure 3.5 and it will change to a button that says *Join with Google Meet* which tells you that it has been configured as a Google Meet meeting.

Figure 3.7

From here you can also click on the copy button to the right of the window as shown in figure 3.7 which will copy the meeting information so you can paste it into an email to send out to the people who you would like to join your meeting.

If you were to click on the *Save* button as seen in figure 3.5 it would just save the meeting on your Google calendar as a standard calendar entry with no Google Meet meeting assigned to it.

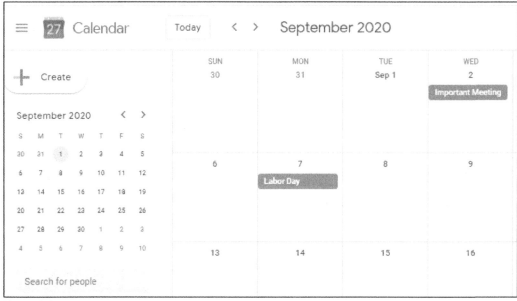

Figure 3.8

If you accidentally save it without making it a Google Meet meeting then you can simply go to that date in your Google Calendar, click on the event and then click on the *Join with Google Meet* button.

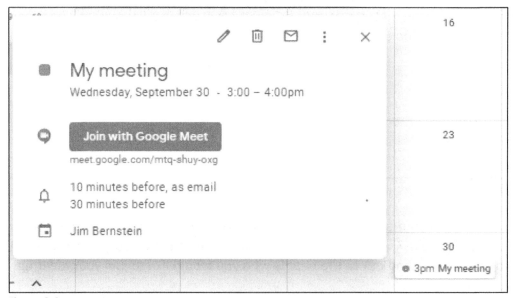

Figure 3.9

Another way to schedule a meeting is to start by going to your Google Calendar and clicking on the date you want to use for the meeting. From here you can enter in the details such as the date and time, attendees and description. Then you can click on the *Add Google Meet video conferencing* button to have your calendar configure a Meet meeting for you. Clicking on the *More options* button will bring up the interface seen back in figure 3.5 where you can fine tune your meeting details.

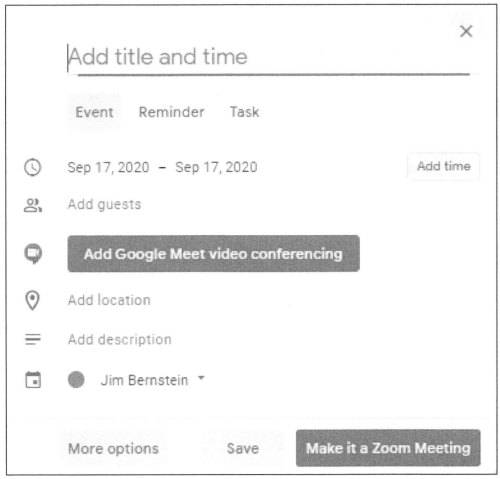

Figure 3.10

Then when the time comes for your reminder, you will get a popup on your computer as seen in figure 3.11 which is how it will look on a computer running Windows 10.

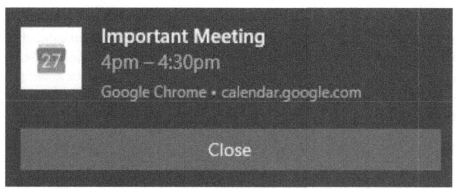

Figure 3.11

Once you have a meeting or meetings scheduled then you can go into your Google Calendar and start your meeting whenever you are ready for it to begin by clicking on the *Join with Google Meet* button.

You can also click on the envelope icon from your calendar entry to send out invitations to other people via email.

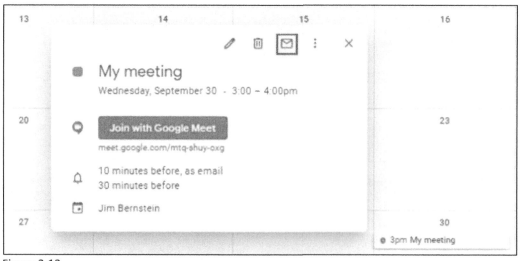

Figure 3.12

Then all you need to do is add your recipients, a subject and a description of what your meeting will be about and then send it on its way. The people you send the invitation to will get an email with a link to your meeting that looks similar to figure 3.14.

Email guests

☑ Send copy to me

👤 Tom Brown ✕ 📋

Add email or name

Subject
Join my meeting

We will be discussing some very interesting topics!|

51 / 2,400

Event information will be included in the message   Cancel   Send

Figure 3.13

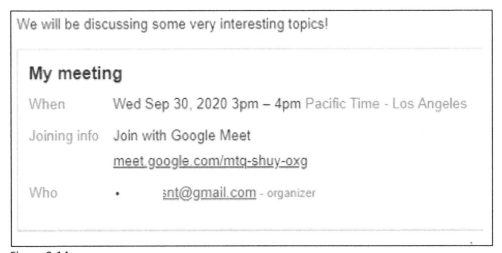

We will be discussing some very interesting topics!

My meeting

When   Wed Sep 30, 2020 3pm – 4pm Pacific Time - Los Angeles

Joining info   Join with Google Meet

                meet.google.com/mtq-shuy-oxg

Who   •   snt@gmail.com - organizer

Figure 3.14

Inviting Others to Your Meeting

When creating meetings, obviously you will want other people to attend or else what's the point of having one, right? Fortunately, it's very easy to invite other people to your meetings right from the Meet interface if you don't want to do it from your calendar or from a scheduled meeting.

When you start a meeting you will be presented with a popup box that will allow you to add people by copying the meeting link that you can then email them (figure 3.15) or if you click on *Add people* you can then manually type in their email addresses as seen in figure 3.16.

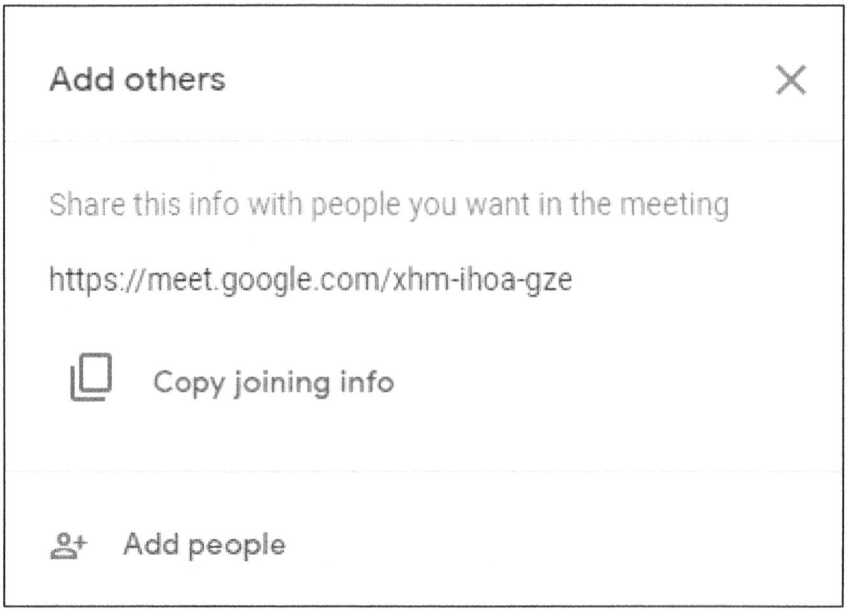

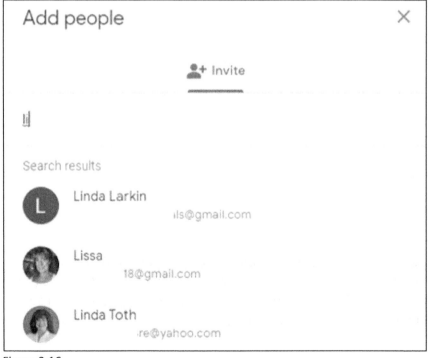

Figure 3.15

Figure 3.16

When typing in email addresses manually, you will notice that as you type, Meet will start to show you email addresses based on the letters you are typing. So rather than having to type the entire address, you can click on the one you want from the suggestion to have it entered in the recipient box.

If you have already started your meeting and wish to invite others then you can click on Meeting details at the lower left of the screen and then you will be able to copy the meeting link and send it out via email, chat or any other method where you can paste the link and send it to someone else.

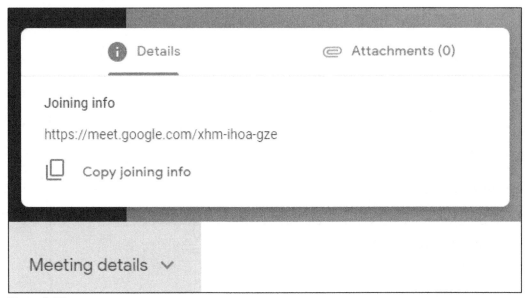

Figure 3.17

Viewing Meeting Participants

If you are hosting meetings with a large number of people you might want to know who has joined your meeting so you can get an idea if anyone is missing or if someone is there that shouldn't be.

To see who has joined your meeting all you need to do is click on the participants' icon at the top right of the screen as seen in figure 3.18. As you can see there is a number 2 next to the icon indicating that there are 2 people currently in the meeting.

Figure 3.18

When you click on the participants' icon you will be shown a listing of who is in your meeting and be able to initiate a chat (discussed next) or even have the ability to invite additional people to your meeting.

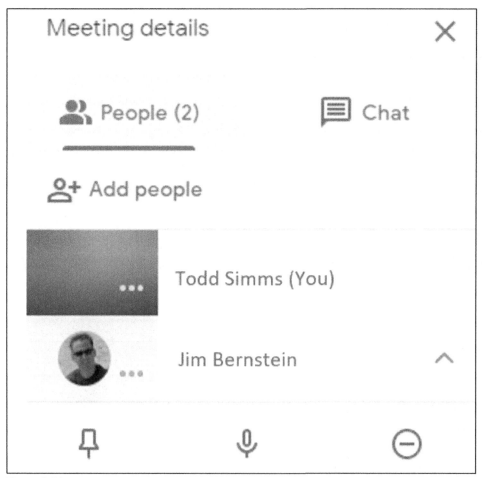

Figure 3.19

When you click on an individual participant you will have three options as shown at the bottom of figure 3.19. The thumbtack option allows you to pin that person to your list which can be used to keep track of them if you have a large number of participants. Only you will see that you pinned someone, and they will not know that you did so.

The microphone can be used to mute someone if they are getting unruly or if they have some background noise that is affecting the audio in your meeting. For privacy reasons, you cannot unmute another person if they are muted.

If you have a case where someone is getting out of hand or shouldn't be in your meeting to begin with then you can click on the circle icon with the line in the middle to remove them from your meeting. Only the event moderator\host can remotely remove another participant.

Chatting

The chatting feature in Meet allows you to send instant messages to everyone so they can read what you have to say rather than interrupting the meeting by talking out of turn for example. It's also a great way to share website links so others can click on them right from the chat box and go to that particular website.

You get to the chat feature the same way you do to see your participants but this time you will click on the chat icon which is to the right of the participant's icon which was shown in figure 3.18

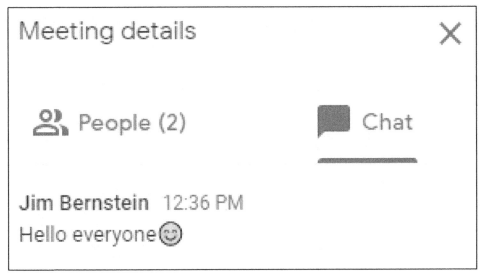

Figure 3.20

Once you are there, all you need to do is type in your message and press enter on your keyboard or click the send button to the right of where you type which looks like a paper airplane icon.

Then everyone in the meeting will be able to see the chat notification as shown in figure 3.21 which they can click on to show any chat messages from other participants.

Figure 3.21

Chapter 4 – Presenting (Screen Sharing)

One of the main reasons for holding online meetings is so you can share information with the other people who are attending your meeting. This comes in very handy when you are unable to make it into the office or if your attendees are all located in different geographic locations.

Sharing your screen is when you allow everyone else on your meeting to see what you are seeing on your own computer\desktop or mobile device. So if you are working on an Excel spreadsheet for example then you can allow others to see your spreadsheet as you are manipulating it.

All of the major online meeting providers such as Zoom and Microsoft Teams allow for screen sharing and some do it better than others. Google Meet also has the ability to share your screen and it works fairly well and will be sufficient for most people.

The Screen Sharing Process
When it comes time to share your screen, or present your screen as Meet calls it, all you need to do is click on the *Present now* button at the lower left of your screen.

Figure 4.1

Then you will get a popup asking you what you would like to share, and you should have 3 choices as seen in figure 4.2.

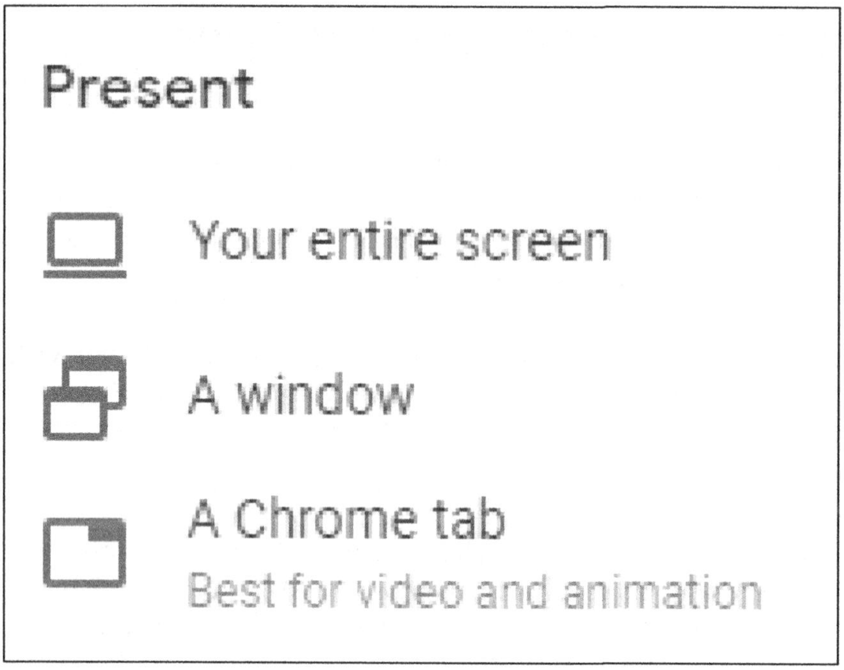

Present

☐ Your entire screen

⧉ A window

☐ A Chrome tab
Best for video and animation

Figure 4.2

Here is what each choice will allow you to do.

- **Your entire screen** – This option will show your attendees everything on your screen as you are seeing it. So if you were to switch from a spreadsheet to a document or to a website you have open in your browser, they will see everything you are doing.

- **A window** – If you would only like your attendees to see a specific program or file that you have open such as a single document then you would choose this option and then you can choose which window you want to share from the programs\files that you have open as seen in figure 4.3.

- **A Chrome tab** – If you use Google Chrome as your web browser then you can choose this option to have Meet share a particular tab that you have open within your browser so you can share a specific website with your participants.

When you are sharing your screen, Meet will give you a notification that you are sharing something and give you an option to pause or stop the sharing as in figure 4.4.

As you start using more Google products you might start to notice that Google likes to integrate their applications to offer increased functionality between them. Another reason they do this to try and push you into using more of their products!

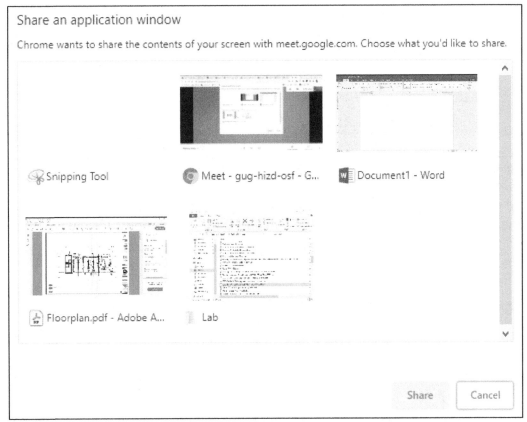

Figure 4.3

> ⏸ meet.google.com is sharing a window.   **Stop sharing**   Hide

Figure 4.4

As you can see, it's very easy to share what you are working on with your attendees and also to fine tune exactly what you want them to see. Some of the other online meeting services might offer a little more in the way of sharing but as I mentioned before, Meet does a good enough job for most users.

Attachments

You might have noticed that when you clicked on Meeting details that there was a section that said Attachments, but it showed 0 attachments and there was no way to add any attachments to your meeting. This is because you need to add any files that you want to share with others from your Google Calendar so they can be accessed by your participants.

Figure 4.4

So if I were to go back to my Google Calendar and edit my meeting by clicking on the pencil icon I can then go back in and add some attachments for my meeting. This can also be done when you create a new meeting.

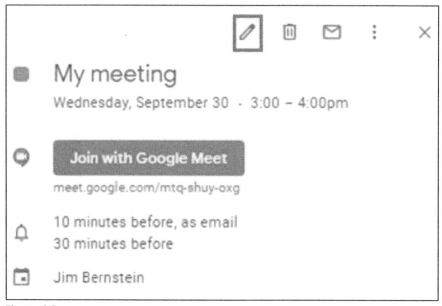

Figure 4.5

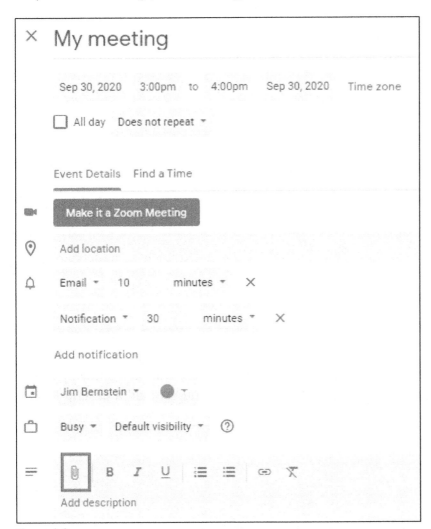

Figure 4.6

When I click on the attachment (paperclip) button I will be given a choice as to where I would like to select my attachments from.

- **Recent** – This will show you files that you have recently worked on.

- **My Drive** – If you use the Google Drive cloud storage service then you can select files that you have stored here.

- **Shared with me** – If others have shared files with you via Google Drive then you can choose those files.

- **Upload** – Here you can upload files that you have stored on your computer.

Figure 4.7

Once you have chosen your files (and click Save), they will then show up in the attachments section of your calendar entry. Then you can add a description for the attachments if desired.

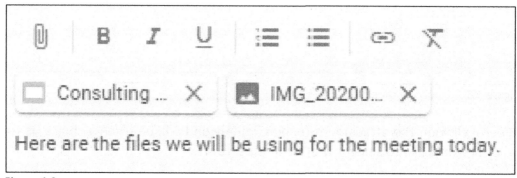

Figure 4.8

When you send out the email invitations, your invitees will be able to open the meeting attachments from the email invitation that you send out to them in case they want to get a preview of what you will be discussing in your meeting. All the person has to do is click on the link for the file they want to open and then they will be able to view it without being in the meeting (figure 4.9).

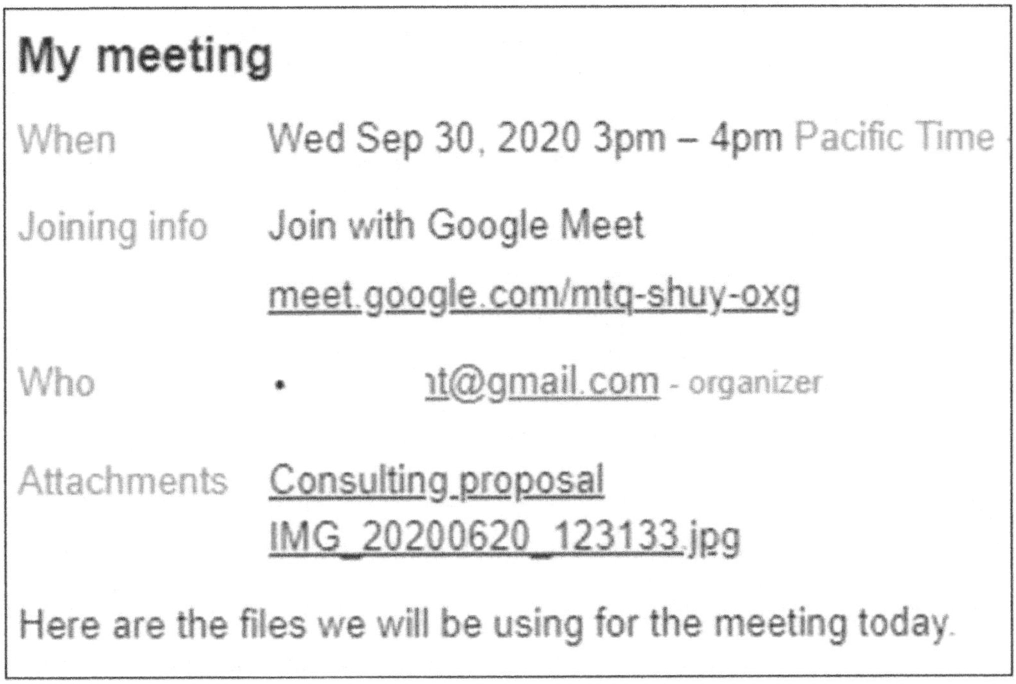

My meeting

When	Wed Sep 30, 2020 3pm – 4pm Pacific Time
Joining info	Join with Google Meet
	meet.google.com/mtq-shuy-oxg
Who	• ıt@gmail.com - organizer
Attachments	Consulting proposal
	IMG_20200620_123133.jpg

Here are the files we will be using for the meeting today.

Figure 4.9

After you add your attachments to your meeting you SHOULD be able to start your meeting and see them under the meeting details and then the attachments section but as of this writing, this feature does not want to work properly. It may also be a case of it being a feature for the Google G Suite version which is a subscription based service that costs money unlike the free version of Meet. I have reached out on the Google forums and to Google themselves but have not been able to find an answer to why this is not working of it is supposed to be a feature of the free version. Hopefully you have better luck than I did!

Chapter 5 – Additional Features

As you can see, Meet is a fairly basic application that gives you the functionality to host online meetings and video calls but lacks some of the bells and whistles that some of the competing services offer.

In this chapter, I would like to go over some of the additional features that you can use to give you some extra functionality while in your meetings. You are not required to use these features for your meetings, but they will come in handy and you will most likely want to take advantage of them.

Captions

The captions feature can be used to translate what you are saying through your microphone into written text that is displayed on the screen for all of your participants to see. That way they can read what you are saying in case it's hard to understand you or if they want to have their sound muted, or don't have sound output on their device for some reason.

To enable the captions feature, all you need to do is click on *Turn on captions* at the lower right hand side of the Meet window.

Figure 5.1

After it is enabled you will see that the box now says *Turn off captions* meaning if you click it again, it will disable the caption feature. Now when you speak into your microphone you will notice that it adds what you are saying as text in the screen for everyone to see (figure 5.2). It actually does a really good job of translating the speech to text and from my experience does a better job than my smartphone does.

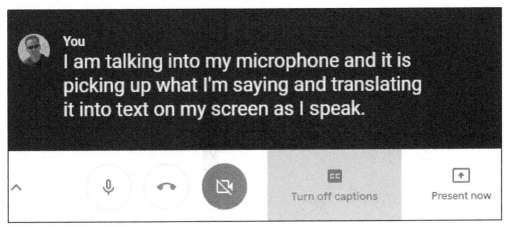

Figure 5.2

If other people are using captions then their text will show up on the screen as well but if you end up with a lot of people using this feature then things will start to look a little messy and it will be hard to keep up with all of the reading!

Participant Views

When you have multiple people (participants) in your meeting, Meet will use its best judgement as to how everyone is displayed on the screen. But if you would like to change how you see others in your meeting then you can choose one of the other options by clicking on the three vertical dots in the lower right corner and then choosing *Change layout* (figure 5.3).

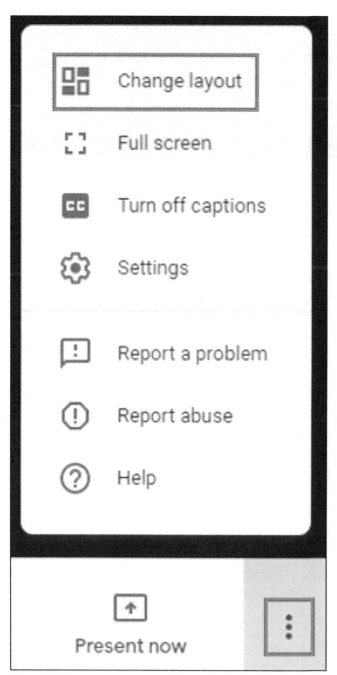

Figure 5.3

Then you will be shown the view options that you have available to choose from as seen in figure 5.4.

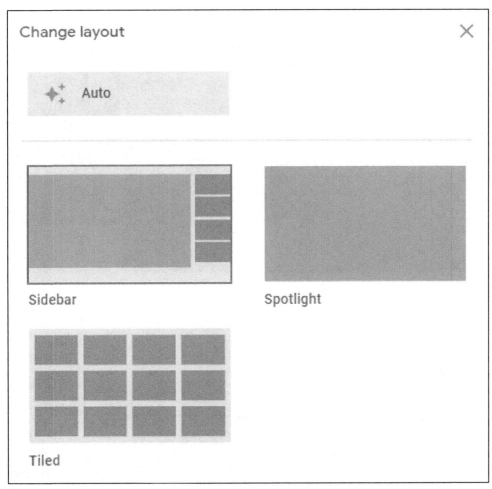

Figure 5.4

The default setting is *Auto* but you also have three other options to choose from.

- **Sidebar** – This option will put the speaker in the middle and have the rest of the participants in smaller windows off to the right side of the screen as shown in figure 5.5 (image courtesy of Google). You will not be able to fit all of your participants in the sidebar if you have too many so keep that in mind.

- **Tiled** – The Tiled view will show everyone in smaller, equal sized windows on the screen as shown in figure 5.6 (image courtesy of Google).

- **Spotlight** – When using the Spotlight view, the person who happens to be speaking will be shown using up the entire screen.

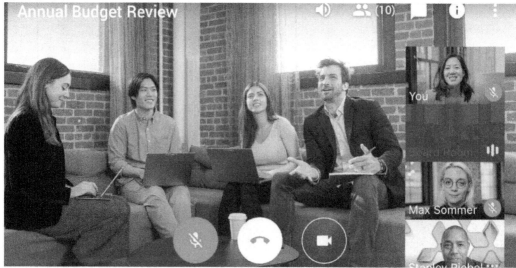

Figure 5.5

Figure 5.6

Adding Whiteboard Capabilities

Unlike some of the more advanced online meeting services like Zoom and Microsoft Teams, Google Meet lacks a whiteboard feature that would normally allow you to draw on the screen as if you were using a whiteboard on your wall.

If you really need this capability then there are ways to work around it even though they are not office Google Meet features. In this section I will be discussing three options that you can check out to add some degree of whiteboard functionality to your meetings.

Google Chrome Canvas
The first app I will be discussing is actually made by Google and is called *Chrome Canvas*. It's a web based whiteboard with limited functionality that you can use for free by going to the Chrome Canvas website (**https://canvas.apps.chrome/**).

Once you are there you can click on the *Get started* button to gain access to the website and the whiteboard.

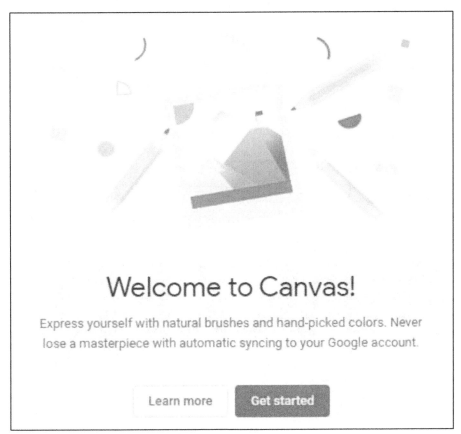

Welcome to Canvas!

Express yourself with natural brushes and hand-picked colors. Never lose a masterpiece with automatic syncing to your Google account.

Learn more   **Get started**

Figure 5.7

Before you start using Canvas you will need to sign in with your Google account and by doing this it will allow you to save your whiteboard drawings so you can view or share them later. Then you can click on *New drawing* to start a new blank drawing or *New from image* to load a picture from your computer to be your background that you can then draw on top of.

Figure 5.8

Once you start a new drawing you can use the various tools like the pencil, pen, marker and eraser as well as change their colors.

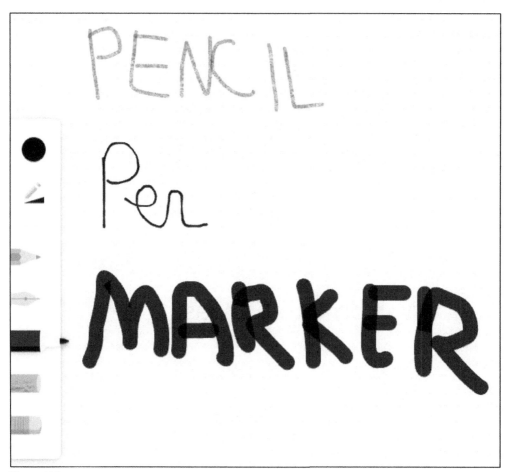

Figure 5.9

Clicking the three vertical dots at the top right of the screen will let you save your drawing as an image file that you can then keep for review purposes or send to other people.

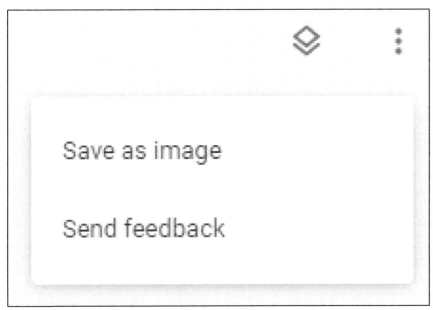

Figure 5.10

Every drawing you create will be saved to your Google account when you go to the Canvas website when you are logged in. You can then edit existing drawings or delete ones that you don't want to keep.

Jamboard
Another option you can use is called Jamboard and once again it's a Google app that you can use via a web browser. It's also used to connect to physical whiteboard devices that connect to your device. These physical whiteboards are for professional situations and can be very expensive.

To start a new Jam as they are called, all you need to do is go to your Google Drive and click on the *New* button, then click on *More* and finally *Google Jamboard*. Then you will be presented with a new Jam as they call it which is essentially a blank whiteboard.

If you are interested in learning more about Google Drive and many of the other Google Apps then you should check out my book titled **Google Apps Made Easy** to learn more! https://www.amazon.com/dp/1798114992

Figure 5.11

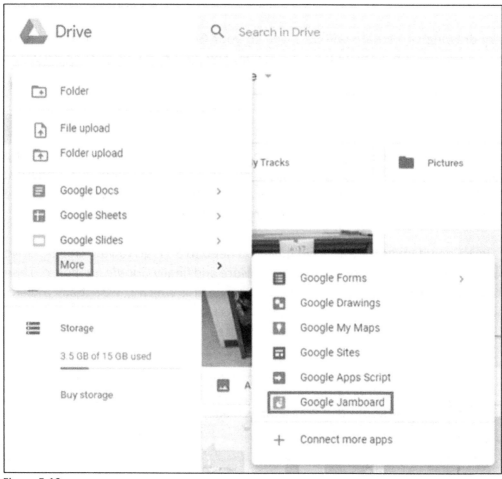

Figure 5.12

From here you can do things such as add images, text and even sticky notes. There are also options to change the background to things such as a solid color or a pattern. If you have the need to have more than one "page" for your whiteboard then you can easily add additional ones to your Jam.

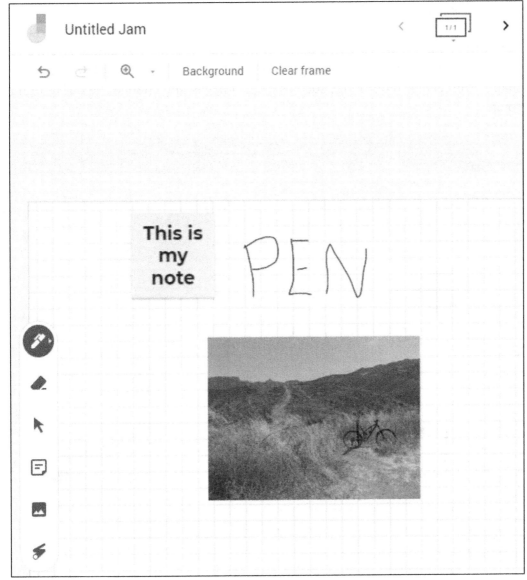

Figure 5.13

Jamboard drawings can also be saved as image files and shared with others online. The. The saving and sharing functionality is a little better than what you get in Canvas but both apps are very similar in regards to what they offer.

Microsoft Paint 3D

One last tool I want to discuss for whiteboard functionality comes included with Microsoft Windows and is very easy to use and can be very effective for your basic whiteboard needs. This program is called *Microsoft Paint 3D* and is the updated version of the classic MS Paint that has been included with Windows pretty much since the beginning.

The newer Paint 3D offers many more features than the old MS Paint program and you can do things such as use pens, markers and crayons as well as add 2D and 3D shapes. You can also do things such as insert images and change the background color.

Figure 5.14

The only downside to using Paint 3D is that it's not an online application and the only way to share your drawings is to save them as an image file or Paint 3D project and then send them others via something like email for example. And if you want to go back to a drawing you will need to make sure it's saved as a Paint 3D Project on your computer so you can open it again.

Chapter 6 – Options and Settings

Just like with most software applications, there are options and settings within Google Meet that you can change to help make the app work better to suit your needs. Although the settings within Meet are fairly basic compared to other meeting applications, it's still a good idea to know what you can change and where you need to go to change it.

There are not too many settings you can change so this will be a very short chapter. Other online meeting services such as Zoom have many settings that can be changed to really customize the way the software works but it appears that Google just wants to keep things simple with Meet.

Audio Settings
The first of the settings that I would like to discuss are the audio settings but before I get into that I need to show you how to access the Meet settings. To get into the settings simply click on the three vertical dots in the lower right hand corner of the screen and then click on *Settings*.

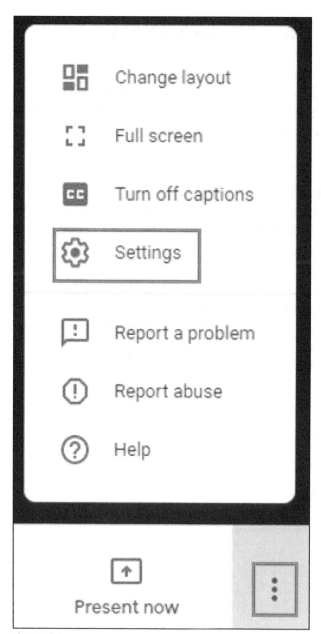

Figure 6.1

The first thing you will see in the Settings area are the *Audio* settings and as you can see from figure 6.2, they are very limited. You have the option of choosing a different microphone or speaker to use in case you have more than one connected to your computer. You can speak into your microphone and watch the dots next to the icon change to test out your microphone before using it in a meeting. You can also click the Test\speaker icon to test out the audio device on your computer.

When doing so, your computer will make a sound letting you know that it is functioning properly.

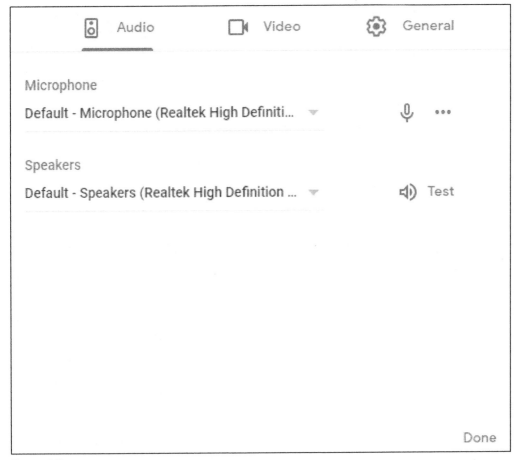

Figure 6.2

Video Settings

Once you have your audio settings configured and working properly you can then click on *Video* to make sure your camera is working and set up the way you like. As you can see in figure 6.3, you can choose from multiple cameras if you have more than one and also see a preview of how things are looking.

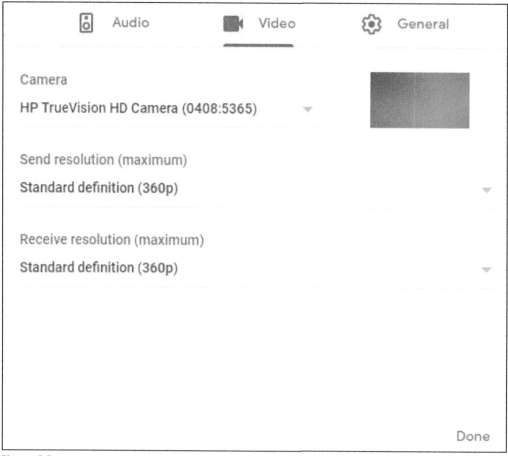

Figure 6.3

You can also change the video resolution if you would like a sharper video image but keep in mind that it will require more bandwidth (faster internet connection) to support higher resolutions but with today's high speed internet it shouldn't be a problem. But for more video calls\meetings the default standard definition should work just fine.

Additional Settings and Help

You might have noticed that there is a *General* settings area with a gear icon next to it but when you click on it there isn't really anything you can do except check the box that says *Report additional diagnostics to help improve this product*. This will most likely send performance and error details about your meetings to Google so they can see how Meet is working so it's up to you if you want to share your information with them or not. You may see additional settings in this area in the future if Google decides to add any.

Speaking of improving the way Meet works, you might have noticed that there is a *Report a problem* choice that you can select after clicking on the three vertical dots at the lower left corner of the screen once again.

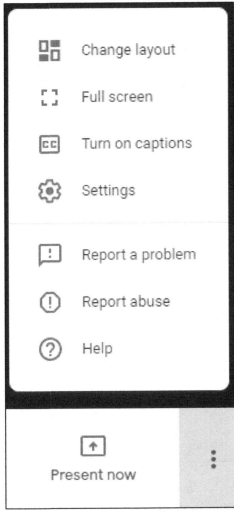

Figure 6.4

This can be used to send Google a report on a specific issue you have found when using the software. Whether or not they will take your report into consideration or even look at it is anyone's guess though!

Another choice from this menu that I want to mention is the one labeled *Report abuse*. If you have someone in your meeting who is doing inappropriate things or even someone who has hijacked your meeting by managing to get their hands on your meeting link then you can report them to Google using this option.

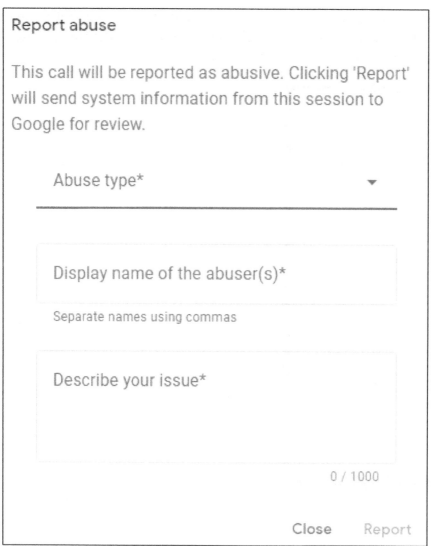

Figure 6.5

Here you can change the abuse type to something that matches the situation such as someone sending spam messages or harassing other users. You can then type in their user name(s) and type in some details about their behavior. Then you can click on *Report* and have it sent off to Google for them to hopefully deal with.

The last thing I would like to cover is the help section that you can access if you have additional questions on how Meet works or how to do something. When you click on the word *Help* as seen in figure 6.4 you will be taken to the Google Meet support website as shown in figure 6.6.

From here you can do things such a read up on various topics from the categories that they have listed on the site or you can type in a question or feature that you would like to learn about from the search box at the top of the screen.

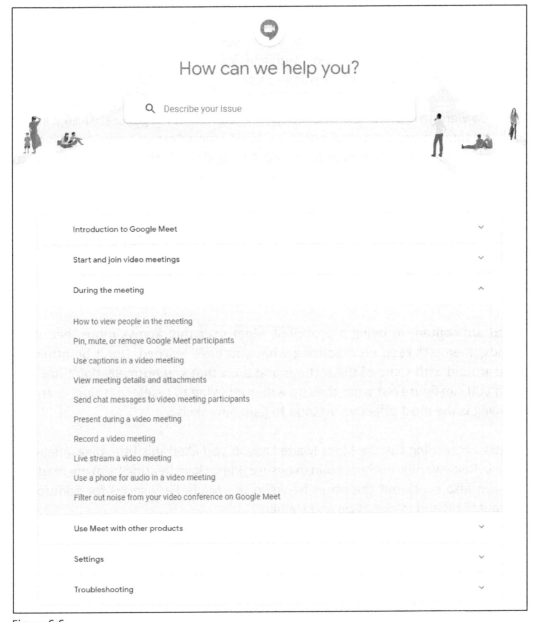

Figure 6.6

For the most part, once you start using Google Meet and poking around the interface you should be able to get the hang of it fairly quickly and be able to host and join meetings with confidence that you will be able to accomplish your goals without running into too many obstacles if any.

What's Next?

Now that you have read through this book and learned how Google Meet works and what you can do with the software, you might be wondering what you should do next. Well, that depends on where you want to go. Are you happy with what you have learned, or do you want to further your knowledge of Meet and online meetings or even take the next step and learn about other online meeting platforms such as Zoom or Microsoft Teams?

If you do want to expand your knowledge and computers in general, then you can look for some more advanced books on basic computers or focus on a specific technology such as Windows or Microsoft Office, if that's the path you choose to follow. Focus on mastering the basics, and then apply what you have learned when going to more advanced material.

There are many great video resources as well, such as Pluralsight or CBT Nuggets, which offer online subscriptions to training videos of every type imaginable. YouTube is also a great source for instructional videos if you know what to search for.

If you are content in being a proficient Meet user that knows more than your friends, then just keep on practicing what you have learned. Don't be afraid to poke around with some of the settings and tools that you normally don't use and see if you can figure out what they do without having to research it since learning by doing is the most effective method to gain new skills.

Thanks for reading Google Meet Made Easy. If you liked this title, please leave a review. Reviews help authors build exposure. Plus, I love hearing from my readers! You can also check out the other books in the Made Easy series for additional, computer-related information and training.

You should also check out my website at **www.onlinecomputertips.com**, as well as follow it on Facebook at **https://www.facebook.com/OnlineComputerTips/** to find more information on all kinds of computer topics.

About the Author

James Bernstein has been working with various companies in the IT field since 2000, managing technologies such as SAN and NAS storage, VMware, backups, Windows Servers, Active Directory, DNS, DHCP, Networking, Microsoft Office, Photoshop, Premiere, Exchange, and more.

He has obtained certifications from Microsoft, VMware, CompTIA, ShoreTel, and SNIA, and continues to strive to learn new technologies to further his knowledge on a variety of subjects.

He is also the founder of the website onlinecomputertips.com, which offers its readers valuable information on topics such as Windows, networking, hardware, software, and troubleshooting. James writes much of the content himself and adds new content on a regular basis. The site was started in 2005 and is still going strong today.

Made in the USA
Coppell, TX
13 December 2020